Ancient Fire
Poems and Translations

Peter Saint-Andre

Ancient Fire

CONTENTS

INVOCATION

Ancient Fire

Sing me, Muse, of your bright sister – small and dark,
They say she was, though I shall never know her.
Her song is lost, yet even her merest shards
    Are a vibrant spark.

She is like a god to me, who sang that song
Of love for what one loves. A pagan was she,
Whose Christian fate it was to burn, her art cut
    Short when night grew long.

Misguided faith I can forgive, but to lose
The greatest of the poets, whose song should live,
I cannot bear. I can but pay her homage:
    Sappho, be my muse

PETER SAINT-ANDRE

STROPHE: SAPPHIC SHARDS

Deathless Aphrodite

Deathless Aphrodite on your lavish throne,
Enchantress, daughter of Zeus: I beg you, queen,
Do not overpower my soul with heartaches
  And hardest troubles,

But come here, if ever at another time
Having heard my voice you paid me attention
And leaving the golden house of your father
  You came to my aid,

Yoking your horse and chariot: gorgeous swift
Sparrows carried you over the coal-black earth,
Thickly whirling their feathers through the middle
  Of heaven's ether.

Swiftly they arrived, and you, O blessed one,
Smiling with your immortal face, you asked for
What I suffered, and why again I call you,
And what in my maddened soul I want most
To happen to me: what dear one shall I now
Persuade to lead you back to her — who, Sappho,
  Has wronged you this time?

Even if she flees, swiftly she will pursue;
If she doesn't receive my gifts, she will give;
If she doesn't love me, swiftly she will love —
Even against her will. So come to my aid,
Release me from my grievous cares, and fulfill
What my heart yearns to be fulfilled: come and be
  My fellow-fighter.

Come Here to Me From Crete

Come here to me from Crete, to your temple,
Where stands your lovely grove of apple trees,
Where holy altars smoke with frankincense;

Here cold water sounds through apple branches,
The ground is all carpeted with roses,
Enchanted sleep falls from shimmering leaves;

Here the field that's grazed by horses is lush
With spring flowers, here the winds sweetly blow
[...]

Here, O goddess, so gracefully you grasp
The golden cup, freely pouring like wine
The nectar all-mixed with our rejoicing.

Some Say

Some say
The most beautiful thing
Over the coal-black earth,
Is an army arrayed
With horses and armor.

I say
The most beautiful thing
Over the coal-black earth,
Is whatever you love
And desire the most.

Easy
It is to make this clear,
For Helen, far besting
All mortals in beauty,
Left the best of all men.

Passion
Drove her, sailing away,
Nor did she remember
Her parents or children
On her way to far Troy.

Now she,
My Anactoria,
Has also gone away [...]
My preference would be

To see
The supple way she walks
And her bright, sparkling face
Than armies of chariots
Or foot-soldiers in arms.

He Seems to Me

He seems to me, that one,
An equal of the gods,
The man fixed there, who sits
Across from you and hears
Close by your voice, your laugh,
Which once so shook my soul.
For as I look on you,
My voice yields up no sound,
My tongue silently shivers,
My skin turns hot with fire,
My eyes give me no sight,
My ears pound their own sound,
A sweat chills over me,
A trembling seizes me,
I'm paler than the reeds,
And in my weakened state,
I'm little short of death.
But all must be endured....

Fragments on Eros

Eros shook my soul like the wind
Attacking the trees on a mountain.

~

Sweetest mother, I lack the power
To strike the loom — I am consumed
With love from slender Aphrodite.

~

Again limb-loosening Eros shakes me;
A helpless crawling thing I am, sweet-bitter.

PETER SAINT-ANDRE

ANTISTROPHE: ODES OF HORACE

I Have Built a Monument

(Odes III.30)

I have built a monument
Which will last more years than bronze,
Which will reach far higher than
That royal pile of Pyramids,
Which gnawing rain and furious
North winds lack power to destroy,
Nor chain of years, nor flight of time.
Oblivion won't be complete,
The greatest part of me will live
Beyond the grasp of greedy death.
I'll prosper on, fed fresh with praise.
For while the priest and silent virgin
Still climb the Capitoline hill,
In places high and places low —
Where the raging Aufidus thunders,
Where Daunus lords it over those
Whose farms are starved of life-rich rain —
Forever I will be proclaimed
As having been the very first
To make the songs of ancient Greece
Dance freely to Italian beats.
Melpomene, accept with pride
The honor you've so richly earned:
Place Delphic laurels on my head.

The Muses' Friend

(Odes I.26)

I am the Muses' friend: I consign all grief
And fear to violent winds on the Cretan sea,
Utterly untroubled by threats besetting
  Some exiled tyrant,

By kings who are feared in the far icy north.
O sweet muse, who delights in the purest springs,
Come bind these sun-filled flowers and weave a crown
  For my Lamia.

Without you, muse, all praise of me is nothing:
So it's all fitting that you and your sisters
Should consecrate it with these fresh strings and a
  Plectrum from Lesbos.

What Shall a Singer Ask of Apollo?

(Odes I.31)

What shall a singer ask of Apollo
While pouring wine from the offering bowl?
Not the fertile cornfields of rich Sardinia;
Not the finest herds of hot Calabria;
Not gold or ivory from far India;
Not the land that's washed away by gentle
Waters from the quiet-flowing Liris.
Let those whom Fate has assigned prune the vines
With Calenian scythes so that some rich
Merchant may drink deeply, from golden cups,
The wine for which he trades Syrian goods
(He's dear to the gods, for three times a year
He ventures on the Atlantic, unscathed) —
My feast is olives, chicory, mallows.
Grant me my health, I pray, let me enjoy
What I have and pass old age with a sound
Mind, with honor, and with my cithara.

A Priest of the Muses

(Odes III.1)

I keep away and loathe the lowly crowd,
I keep a sacred silence: for I am
A priest of the Muses and I sing songs
Never heard before to virgins and boys.
Great rulers are feared by their subject-flocks,
But high over them is the rule of Jove,
Famed for his triumph over the Giants,
Changing all by a move of his eyebrow.
It's true that one man plants greater vineyards,
That one candidate in the Campus is
Of nobler descent while another is
Of greater fame and worth, and a third has
A bigger crowd of followers — yet Fate,
With blind justice, decides the end of high
And low alike: the urn stirs every name.
To one above whose neck the drawn sword hangs,
Sicilian feasts hold no sweet taste, nor will
Songs of birds or citharas let him sleep —
Yet gentle dreams do not shun peasant homes,
Shady riverbanks, and breezy valleys.
One who desires no more than his needs
Is not disturbed by stormy seas and the
Raging onset of setting Arcturus
Or rising Haedus, not by the hail that
Attacks his vines, nor by an estate that
Disappoints him, the fruit-trees now blaming
Floods, now field-parching stars, now harsh winter.
Or look here: shunning land, crowds of workers,
The contractor, and the owner himself
Lay their stones in the water, and fishes
Are confined by pilings built in the deep;
Yet fear and threats plague the proprietor,
And gloomy trouble besets his bronze-beaked

Trireme and settles behind his horsemen.
If Phrygian marble, brilliant purples,
Falernian wines, and Persian spices
Can't comfort one who's in pain, then why build
A hall with pillars in the latest style?
Why switch my Sabine vale for troubling wealth?

You Shun Me

(Odes I.23)

You shun me like a fawn that's seeking
Through trackless hills her mother peeking,
    Ill with fear of the woods and breeze;

When pliant leaves the spring winds rustle
Or lizards through the bushes bustle
    She trembles in her heart and knees.

But not I like the tiger savage
Or wild lion seek to ravage:
    So come, you're ripe a man to please.

Deep With Snow

(Odes I.9)

You see how white Soractus stands there deep with snow
And how the laboring woods struggle to support
Their burden, and the rivers stand stock still with frost.

So drive out the cold, Thaliarchus, piling logs
High on the fire, and bring out in abundance
The four-year-old wine contained in that Sabine jar.

Leave all else to the gods, for neither cypresses
Nor ancient wild ash trees are much disturbed when
They scatter the warring winds over raging seas.

Do not bother asking what tomorrow will bring,
Consider as gain whatever days fortune grants —
Do not spurn sweet loves and dances while you're still
young,

While yet you're flourishing and capricious old age
Has not yet arrived. So come, let's seek out the town,
With low-voiced whispering at the appointed hour

Under the stars, the tell-tale laughter of a girl
Who's hiding in the farthest corner, and the pledge
That's torn from her arm or finger, not unyielding.

The Snows Have Fled

(Odes IV.7)

The snows have fled, already grass returns
To the fields and leaves return to the trees.
Earth turns her changes; rivers are slowing.
Grace with her Nymphs and twin sisters ventures
Forth naked to lead her bands of dancers.
The year and the hour that steal away
The nourishing day give us their warning:
"Don't hold out hope for immortality."
The Zephyr lessens the cold, the Summer
Tramples the Spring but then is overturned
When fruit-bearing Fall has poured forth its crops;
Soon enough dead winter returns again.
Swift moons will heal the heavenly damage —
But when finally we have gone down where
Good Aeneas, rich Tullus, and Arcus
Have gone — we will become mere dust and shade.
Who knows if the gods will add to our sum
Tomorrow? The only thing that escapes
Your heir is what you've added to your soul.
When you have died and Minos has given
His judgment, nothing, Torquatus — not birth
Nor eloquence nor worth — restores your life.
Diana can't release Hippolytus
From darkness; Theseus lacks the power
To burst the chains of dear Perithoös.

Keep a Tranquil Mind

(Odes II.3)

Remember when times are difficult to
Keep a tranquil mind, when times are good to
Keep yourself from becoming overjoyed,
Dellius who is yet to face your death,

Whether you will live always in sadness
Or on festal days in a far-off field
Reclining there you will find delight in
A famed vintage of Falernian wine.

Why do the tall pine and the white poplar
So love to join their foliage to make
Inviting shade? And why does the rushing
Water press through the river's winding banks?

Bring along wines, perfumes, and the too-brief
Flower that blooms upon the lovely rose
While your good fortune and our youth allow,
And the dark-spun threads of the three Sisters.

You will leave your boughten lands and country
House, which is washed by the river Tiber —
You will leave them, and some heir will acquire
All the wealth you have piled up so high.

Whether you're rich from an old family
Or you are poor and sleep beneath the stars,
It makes no difference at the very end:
For pitiless Orcus will have your soul.

Each of us is gathered to the same place:
Every lot is turned in the urn of Fate,

The god who will come forth and place each one
In the skiff of Styx, never to return.

The Fleeting Years

(Odes II.14)

Alas, my Postumus, the fleeting years
Will fall away, nor will piety cause
Delay to wrinkles or to advancing
Old age or to indomitable death.

Let's say you were to sacrifice a bull
Each day, still you couldn't placate tearless
Pluto, who with his waves has imprisoned
Both thrice-strong Geryon and Tityos —

Those are the waves, my friend, that you must cross
Along with all who thrive on the earth's gifts,
Whether we are kings or wretched peasants.
In vain would we try to avoid cruel Mars

And the mercurial disturbances
That course across the Adriatic Sea —
In vain throughout the autumn will we fear
The south wind, so harmful to our bodies.

We needs must see the wandering, sluggish
Cocytos and the infamous offspring
Of Danaus and the son of Aeolus:
Sisyphus damned to his ceaseless toil.

We needs must leave behind the earth and home
And our pleasing spouse. And none of those trees
That you tend will follow you, its short-lived
Master, except the reviled cypress.

A worthier heir will guzzle the wine
You guard now with a hundred keys: for he

Will drench the pavement with your best — more fine
Than that on which the highest priests do feast.

It's Better to Live

(Odes II.10)

It's better to live, Licinius, neither
Always pressing out on the deep nor, trembling
And cautious, hugging overly close to the
    Dangerous shoreline.

The power who cherishes the golden mean
Safely avoids the squalor of a hovel
And discreetly keeps away from a palace
    That excites envy.

Most often it's the huge pine that is shaken
By the wind, and the highest towers that fall
The greatest fall, and the tops of mountains that
    Attract the lightning.

Hopeful in adversity, apprehensive
In prosperity is the heart that prepares
Well for either fate. Zeus brings the winter, but
    Also takes it back.

For even if right now times are bad, they won't
Ever be that way: for Apollo doesn't
Always tense his bow, but sometimes he inspires
    The silent Muses.

When the straits you sail have narrowed, show yourself
To be undaunted and bold — yet also be
Wise and tuck your sails when they're swelled by too
strong
    A following wind.

This Aegean Storm

(Odes III.29)

Maecenas, descended from Etruscan kings,
Smooth wine not yet opened and blooming roses
And fragrant hair oils have long been ready
   For you at my house.

Break free from all hindrances: do not always
Contemplate the humid Tibur, Aefula's
Sloping fields, and the ridge of that parricide
   Old Telegonus;

Forsaking loathsome wealth and sky-high power,
Shaking your head at the smoke and wealth and noise
Of decadent Rome, I urge you now to leave:
   For change is pleasant,

And a simple dinner at a peasant's small
Hut all lacking in fine purple tapestries
Loosens the troubled brow of the richest man.
   And see already:

Andromeda's shining father shows forth his
Secret fire; Procyon and the harsh star
Of Leo rage, and the sun brings back the days,
   Drought-filled, without rain;

The shepherd with his sluggish flock seeks out shade
And stream and the wild brambles of savage
Silvanus, and the quiet banks lack even
   An unsteady breeze.

Yet you worry about the health of the State;
Troubled by the City, you're anxious about

ANCIENT FIRE

The Seres and Cyrus-ruled Bactra and the
  Fractious Scythians.

Wisely the god suppresses the outcome of
Future times in darkest night, and he laughs if
Mortals are disturbed by that which is beyond
  Their proper orbit.

Take care to deal clearly with what's before you —
The rest is carried along like a river:
Now gliding calmly within its channel down
  To the Tuscan sea,

Now churning gnawed rocks and uprooted tree-trunks
And cattle and homes until the surrounding
Woods and hills resound with noise when the fierce flood
  Roils the placid stream.

Joyous and self-possessed is the life of he
Who each day can say: "I have lived — tomorrow
The Father may fill the sky with black storm-clouds
  Or purest sunshine,

Yet even so he can't upset what is past:
He can't complete or alter or make undone
Whatever the fleeting hour has produced."
  For haughty Fortune,

So pleased with her cruel affairs and stubbornly
Playing her games, keeps shifting around all her
Dubious honors, smiling now on me and
  Now on someone else.

I praise her while she stays. Yet when she spreads her
Too-swift wings, I give back what she has granted

And wrapped in my strength I seek out poverty,
   Honest and bereft.

It's not my way, when the southern gales roar out
Of Africa, to make abject prayers and
Votive offerings to strike a bargain lest
   My exotic wares

Should add to the wealth of the rapacious sea;
It's then that the gods and a favoring breeze
Carry me and my two-oared skiff safely through
   This Aegean storm.

You Who Measured the Sea

(Odes 1.28)

You who measured the sea, the earth, and the
    numberless sands,
You, Archytas, are now confined in a small mound of dirt
Near the Matine shore, and what good does it do you
    that you
Attempted the mansions of the skies and that you
    traversed
The round celestial vault — you with a soul born to die?

For these have perished: Tantalus, the father of Pelops,
Guest of the gods; Tithonus, scattered to the far-off winds;
Minos, privy to the secrets of Jove; Pythagoras,
Son of Panthous, held by Tartarus, consigned to Orcus
Not once but twice, who witnessed Trojan times
    by taking down
The shield and who conceded to dark death nothing at all
But his sinews and skin — and I know you consider him
No mean judge of nature and truth. A common
    night awaits
Us all, and in the end we must all tread the path of death.

Some are offered by the Furies to bloody Mars as sport;
Sailors are devoured when they go out on voracious seas;
Mixed corpses of young and old are densely packed
    together;
No head escapes harsh Proserpina. I've been submerged in
Illyrian waves by Orion's swift friend, the south wind.

So, sailor, don't spite me, don't be sparing with
    shifting sands,
Grant instead a little to my unburied bones and skull —
Then may you stay safe whatever the east wind
    vents against
Hesperian waves when Venusian woods are beaten back,
May a great reward flow down to you from Jove
    and Neptune.

Would you make light of committing a wrong
    that might bring harm
To your innocent children? For chance may yet deny you
Due justice and bring you outrageous fortune:
    in which case
My request would not go unrewarded, nor would any
Atonement release you. Though you're in a hurry, the wait
Is short: scatter three handfuls of sand and scurry away.

Pluck the Day

(Odes I.11)

Don't seek, my friend, we cannot say
What end's in store for you, for me:
Don't trust in vague astrology.
Better to shoulder what will be,
Whether you soon will die, or stay
To watch the shore exhaust the sea.
Drink some wine while your hours flee,
Put small trust in posterity,
And prune your hopes — but pluck the day.

PETER SAINT-ANDRE

EPODE: POEMS

In the Garden

Encampment River Trail, May 27th, 2000

In the garden of my life
I'm done with envy, done with strife.
I cultivate my natural joys
Far from this culture's fearful noise.

Congress hall and marketplace,
Fame's small change and honor's race,
Academe's cold, haughty tower –
Have no meaning, hold no power.

Letting go of shoulds and oughts,
I concentrate on greener thoughts
And find as I fulfill my soul
That things spin calmly in control –

That though events conspire still,
They tend to bend toward my will.
No greater cause achieves the measure
Than that of my own reasoned pleasure.

The Measure

Encampment River Trail, October 7th, 2000

A million grains lie in the glass:
The hours that fate may let me pass,
The hours of striving or of rest
(What at that moment I deem best).

Half of the grains wait in the top,
Half of the grains lie where they've dropped,
One grain alone moves as I live:
The hour that's full of what I give.

This hour can seem to last a day
If I but let my powers play
And give what's of my deepest core:
Thought, choice, and action – nothing more.

Yet what for me is nothing less
Are powers mixed with interest
That long and deep in me abides
Where life and nature coincide.

It's here that, when attention's strong,
Each moment seems an hour long,
The flow of time is one with pleasure,
And life achieves its natural measure.

Cobalt

My friend is a cobalt poetry goddess:
She turns her phrases with a quiet power
And dances among her words with style and grace,
  Like Sappho herself.

But she's often, so often, blue: the color
Of the twilight sky, deep and clear, bordering
On the blackest night, yet never losing hold
  Of the light of day.

Sometimes I wish I could brighten her a shade
Or two – make her azure or cerulean.
But then I know I'd never want to change her
  Blue poetic soul.

Troubadour

I write no wondrous stories
Of mankind's vast potential;
I sculpt no human glories
Of what I deem essential.

Mine's a smaller, subtler art
Made of separate arts combined:
Music lets me voice my heart,
Poems let me sing my mind,

But a song's the wedded bliss
Of consummated pleasure
Where my soul and mind can kiss
In free melodic measure.

Liaison D'Etre

The glow of joy does not consist
In the absence of pain and fear:
I measure not my happiness
By the lack of life's negation.
In love's intimate relation
(Than which all other bonds are less),
I've found my other hemisphere
And a reason that I exist.

No Exit

If hell is other people,
As all the gloomsters say,
Then emphatic I agree:

For heaven's other people –
And the closer we lie together
The nearer my god to thee.

Moving Violation

When I heard the news, I practically choked:
My poetic license had been revoked!
It seems that the Central Poetry Board
Decided it was over me they'd lord
By taking away my avocation,
From which I gain no remuneration.

I found their reasoning convoluted,
They found my reaction less than muted:
I vowed not to go from better to worse
By writing any of their fine free verse!
I'll take my metrical lines underground
Before I make verse without sense or sound.

But worst was the "crime" that incited this measure:
They claimed I'd been giving my audience pleasure!

On a Visit to the Musée Rodin

Although I know no French, the usher's
    glare is universal:
"Look but do not touch." Yet can one know
    the passion of the kiss
Just by looking? The eyes aren't enough;
    neither are the hands.

I need no reminder, yet here
    it is: in comes a girl,
Stark blind, her family leading her from
    room to room. I watch —
Roiled by envy, wakened by pity,
    held by fascination.

Her gentle warm hands move slowly
    over the cold unmoving
Marble, changed brusquely by its maker
    from unfeeling stone
To these violent images of longing,
    love, living passion.

In her darkness she has a way
    to know that's not allowed
To me. I sneak a touch while the usher's
    turned but it is
As nothing to her caress.
    Once again, authorities

Enforce the dualism of eye and hand.
    Why can't we join
The light of sight and touch?
    It's what we need so we can gain
An understanding of the kind
    that does not end at stone.

Indivisible

Imagine if you were a number:
Which would you choose to be?
Something firm and solid, like two,
Or something odd, like three?

Zero would be numeric slumber,
The life of *i*, complex;
The air of million might entice you,
Or largest googolplex.

Perhaps you'd be the one and only,
Lost in self-absorption;
Perhaps forsake the whole adventure,
Only be a portion.

I'd risk a life that might be lonely,
But mine in all its time:
I'd open myself up to censure
And choose to be a prime.

The Problem of the One and the Many

(A Serious Nonsense Poem)

We are all familiar, I should say,
    with the way geese gaggle,
Bees swarm, and oxen yoke — the way
    that sheep and seagulls straggle
When they unwisely stray from their appointed flock.

But do you have an inkling of
    the strange and wondrous habits
Of creatures as divergent as
    rhinoceri and rabbits?
Animals guard secrets their fancy names unlock....

To begin, we know that a group
    is made of ones who muster,
And animals acquire
    curious names when they cluster —
Like the nightingales, who en masse become a watch.

Watches of birds, though, I dare say,
    aren't nearly so strange
As troops of hopping kangaroos
    that turn out on the range,
Or holy exaltations of ecstatic larks!

But turn from sacred to profane:
    think of the lowly crow,
Whose group is called a murder! And the elks,
    who numbered show
Themselves to be a gang — yet still they roam our parks!

Litters of piglets, pods of seals,
    or turtles in a bale:
Shall we tie them with strings of ponies,
    set them out for sale —
On a bed of oysters, for optimum display?

The words are stuck like knots of toads,
    to tell me who I am,
How I should live and travel: if grouped
    like whales in a gam
Or alone, like a needle in a stack of hay....

Companies of parrots may be
    founded by one who dares,
Schools of fish or bands of monkeys
    started by one who cares;
The peace of nations dreamt by doves who league in dules.

Hens and chicks, so I've heard, have
    tendencies to brood and clutch;
The hogs just drift, the hares are down,
    and foxes skulk so much
They've lost their craft at leaping over spans of mules.

See the mustering of the storks,
    and vicious hordes of gnats!
Hounds are mute and woodcocks fall
    'midst the clutter of the cats
While the herons' siege runs strong, sounder than the
swine.

But hark, glad tidings of magpies!
    For finches love to charm:
Bouquets of pheasants (they're aware)
    can surely do no harm;
Sparrows play gracious host, and cast their hawks like
wine.

Pride, as all but lions know,
    is widely counted a sin —
Plagues of locusts on your house
    if you let such vices in
As peacock ostentation, and the sloth of bears.

What can one build? Perhaps a nest,
    of rabbits or of vipers!
Or routes of wolves for trips of goats,
    safe from the tribes of snipers,
Where cattle drove in fear of dragons in their lairs!

Build and build again: rafters of turkeys,
    colonies of ants:
Seek the aid of an elephant herd
    to help you make your chance,
Ignore the starlings' murmurations while you're young....

What can we learn from these odd terms
    against which you may rail,
From teams of horses and ducks,
    coveys of partridge and quail?
The question, I'm sure, is on the tip of your tongue:

      Am I part of a swarm or clan,
      Mere member of some coterie?
      Perhaps, perhaps, am I a man —
      Alone, myself, uniquely me?

Urban Haiku

Old woman crossing.
Two thin legs and a walker.
Good it's a long light.

~

Orange city glow
Reflected from clouds above
Bathes the swirling snow.

~

There's no foundation
All the way along the line:
Broadway crazy man.

~

Top-down white Corvette
Blaring down Fifth Avenue.
Six below zero.

~

Fighting traffic noise
Underneath a cherry tree
Practicing bagpipes.

~

Trees as thin as poles
Struggle up through sidewalk holes.
How many will live?

~

Around Columbus,
Like the pigeons overhead,
Taxis keep circling.

~

She has no home but
Her nails are always polished,
Waiting for the bus.

~

Summer in the park:
Homeless men spend warm bright days
Sleeping in the shade.

~

Taxis, trucks, and cars
Intertwine without touching...
A delicate dance.

~

Flapping and whirling
Like a streetwise break dancer,
A pigeon's death-throes.

~

A sea of silver
Clouds below, except the tips
Of two white towers.

~

Deep in her smartphone,
Turning the corner she steps
Deep in wet cement.

~

Countless lonely drops
Joined against their will: mighty
Rivers of traffic.

The Art of the Fugue

How these twelve notes soar and tumble,
Calming my soul in streams of sound.
As lines entwine and themes embrace,
Bracing logic dissolves my cares.

Calming my soul in streams of sound,
Bach weaves his magic mastery.
Bracing logic dissolves my cares;
Creation fills me up with wonder.

Bach weaves his magic mastery
As lines entwine and themes embrace.
Creation fills me up with wonder:
How these twelve notes soar and tumble!

Drought

Acorn-pummeled, the house withstands
The hail of overhanging oaks,
Whose outstretched arms had once stood guard,
Whose dried-up fruit lies deep now on the yard.

Likewise, the verdure of the lawn
(Green rug unfurled to greet the world)
Has turned to tawny brown and bare
Except where crabgrass clings, like tufts of hair.

Though droopy plants are nodding off
And parched earth cries for dew and rain,
The oaks stand strong (their roots run deep)
And life is merely lying low, asleep.

Ivy, My Enemy

There's something quite creepy about ivy
That makes it seem all too alivey:
The slithering mass of it climbs up your house
And clings to your stone or your brick;
Its feet are like glue and its stalk grows as thick
As a snake in your garden that's swallowed a mouse.

On the ground, I suppose, the plant's not such a pest —
But when it climbs, my loathing cannot be expressed.
No, I'm never afraid to assert my opinion
About this green menace of the vast plant dominion:
Though some people say that the vine has its worth,
I'd just as soon see it removed from the earth!

Editor

There's nothing that's quite as horrific
as an editor's pen prolific
marking off which word, which phrase, which page
survives unscathed the editor's rage.
['Rampage', perhaps, is more specific. – Ed.]

You'll start to feel the imposition
of add and cut and transposition,
you'll start to fight for your wordy dream
against those changes that make you scream....
Confronted with his erudition
your protest ends up in contrition.

Eventually you'll drop resistance,
you'll change it all at his insistence,
in this and each and every instance.
And all of this madness for a fee –
you'll dearly wish that he just could be
edited right out of existence!

Fond Wish

Somewhere in the mountains in the
    Wilds of Wyoming,
I'll find some land and make my stand
    And finally end my roaming.
I'll bide my time by the high tree line
    Where the mountains meet the sky.
I'll spend each season in joy and reason,
    And live free till I die.

Crossroads

(after José Ortega y Gasset)

When you finally arrive
   at the crossroads of your life
Don't plunge on blindly through,
   but stop there: inquire deeply
Into yourself and come to know
   the force of your ideal,
Shine great light on your vocation —
   and only then move on.

Jesus in Atlantis

I never claimed to be the Christ,
The son of God, savior of man,
A worker of wonders,
The ender of plunder —
Martyred and anointed,
Divinely appointed
To cleanse all living men of sin.

Such sin I did not recognize:
Violations of long-dead rules.
I brooked no division,
No unnatural fission;
I sought one congregation,
One fellowship of nations,
One home on earth for all to live in.

Upon my death they brought me here:
The home of heroes, not of saints.
At first I didn't understand
Just why this was my final land,
Or why my death upon a cross
Had been a world entire's loss,
How sweet the fruits were of my search.

Slowly, slowly I came to see
The meaning of my too-brief life:
Why some of those I taught did shun
The man I was to make god's son,
And why it was they lost their way
Amidst a crowd of gods and strayed
From simple truths to build a church.

Now every year brings fresh reports
Of violence done (and in my name!)

To what I held divine:
The heart and soul and mind
Of every sacred living man —
And not the so-called higher plans
Of gods above and kings below.

I never lusted for the power
That kings and gods and rulers hold;
I wanted but to teach,
Not even quite to preach,
To live with those who'd share
My way of being, bare
Of pretense, falseness, envy, show.

Oh would that I could intervene
And live with men a second time,
As some think is prophesy:
I'd straighten out my legacy —
Although not as they imagine —
For I would wipe away the sin
That lies deep on my land of birth.

The Christians with their hundred sects,
Even their many heretics,
Came to love authority
Of the kind that murdered me,
Lost their love for that thing —
The human soul — that brings
Good will to men and peace on earth.

Reflections on My Father's Life

September 2, 1999

> As the generations of leaves,
> So the generations of men.
> Down to earth the wind shoots the leaves,
> But forest trees burst forth again
> In the hour when spring is born:
> So one generation of men
> Dies off while another grows strong.
> *The Iliad, VI.146-149*

As the generations of leaves,
So the generations of men.
Yet what's the value of one leaf?
Can it be just to grow the stem?
I think not, but I'm not sure why:
For if I say, as I am wont,
That meaning's made whenever I
Create some value in the world,
Then it would seem the worth of one
Is only in his strength to serve,
To build the beam and build the bough
So others yet may bud and grow
And, having built, may fall to earth
When winter of their time has come.

But so to speak ignores the joy
And pride that comes from bringing new
And unique value to the world
Or keeping whole what's come before,
For sake of others and oneself.
For there's no conflict here: we each
Pursue an interest in the good
Through single acts that are yet whole

And so create without intent
A world that's better for us all.

Thus my father lived: he healed men
Who fought in war then fought again
To gain their health; he sought to save
The land he loved and to preserve
A life long lost through buildings that
The farmers made before our time
(He tried to keep their virtues, too:
Straight honesty with all he knew);
He kept his wife till death did part
And raised four children, all with love
And joy in that most awesome task.

A leaf has fallen from the tree:
And all I ask is that he gain
A due amount of honor from
The ones he touched and left behind.
A leaf has fallen from the tree:
He lived with pride, he lived with joy,
And we who gather here today
Are better for his having lived.

Paying for Shade

Paying for shade,
I herd branches,
Leaves, and needles
Across the lawn —
An advancing
Line of debris,
The jetsam of
Apple and spruce.

An early snow
Means that water
And ice are mixed
In, that I'm late
To garbage bags
And rakes — late to
Gathering this year's
Harvest of death.

Yet with this slough
Cleared away, there's
Room now for the
Sun to provide
What winter warmth
It can, then melt
The snows and burst
The buds of spring.

An old woman
Passes — I smile
And wave, yet her
White hair and my
Pile of fallen
Leaves remind me

Of those I loved
Who now are gone.

PETER SAINT-ANDRE

Looking up at the Sky

December 22, 1999

My friend, this solstice moon reminds me
    to look up at the sky –
The brightest moon in a hundred years,
    they say, but right now I
Can't see the features I like best
    for all this blinding light:
The things my father taught to me
    on moonless winter nights
When we would walk up to Clifton Park
    (where summers I played ball)
And peer at the deep of space to find
    the Dippers large and small,
The twins, the bull, Orion's Belt, but
    most of all the Queen's Chair,
My favorite since harder to find
    and closer to my scale
And the scale of my father's love –
    my eye pursues it even still
Among the million numberless stars,
    the stars that I feel will,
Fighting distance, connect me to you,
    to my passed father's life,
To the numberless millions who lived
    on earth before my time,
To the numberless more who'll live here
    once I'm gone – or who may,
For all I know, not live here at all
    but venture out away
Into space, expand the home of man –
    for them the stars will be
Their park (will they play with comets as
    I played ball?) – yet I see

In my mind's eye that sometimes they'll look back
    at where the earth must lie
And feel as I do when, thinking of you,
    I look up at the sky.

ENVOI

The Course of the Sun

How high, we ask, has the sun yet climbed?
We wonder, hope, but do not know.
No other star we can see so shines,
And yet perhaps it's only show.

It can seem our star has risen far
At some times and in some respects;
But then past glory or future hope
Becomes all that our world reflects.

Except the troubled ascent of man
The world's not seen a star like this,
That rises, and falls, to rise again –
Abyss to bliss to precipice.

Yet looking closely the mind discerns
That, even when our sun grows dark,
In the molten core a fire burns,
Ignited by an ageless spark.

For Further Exploration

No book stands alone. The poems and translations here have been influenced by many sources: the Greek of Sappho (whose beauty I have been unable to match in my English renderings), the Latin of Horace, and various other poets I knew and liked at the time I wrote these poems, such as Andrew Marvell, A.E. Housman, and Theodore Roethke. One can also find the imprint of contemporary poets I admire, especially Timothy Steele, Dana Gioia, Dick Davis, Rhina Espaillat, A.E. Stallings, and John Enright.

Since I wrote these poems and made these translations in the 1990s, I have immersed myself in the work of less formal poets, such as Walt Whitman, Emily Dickinson, and Langston Hughes. Although I have set Hughes's long poem *Freedom's Plow* to music, I have not yet written any poems in a more free-form style.

I would not compare myself to any of the foregoing poets in stature or quality, but I recommend their works without reservation for both craft and content.